THE CHOCOLATE BOOK

SARA PERRY

ILLUSTRATED BY BEN GARVIE

CHRONICLE BOOKS SAN FRANCISCO

To Mark Wheaton, a creative cook, a far-away friend, and best of all, my brother.

Library of Congress Cataloging in Publication Data

Perry, Sara.
    The chocolate book / by Sara Perry :
    illustrated by Ben Garvie.
        p.   cm.
    Includes index.
    ISBN 0-8118-0246-9
    1. Cookery (Chocolate)   I. Title.
TX767.C5P47   1992
641.6′374—dc20   91-47205
                                CIP

Printed in Hong Kong.

Editing: Catherine Gleason
Consulting: Emily Moore
Book and cover design: Julie Noyes Long

Distributed in Canada by Raincoast Books, 112 East Third Ave. Vancouver, B.C. V5T 1C8

10   9   8   7   6   5   4   3   2   1

Chronicle Books
275 Fifth Street
San Francisco, CA 94103

CONTENTS

ODE TO CHOCOLATE

Chocolate as we know it today is a far cry from the cold, peppery drink handed to Cortez in 1519 by the Aztec Emperor Montezuma. This was not sweet revenge. This was a divine potion to celebrate the second coming of Quetzalcoatl, the fair-skinned Aztec god of wisdom, knowledge and *chocolate*.

Xocoatl, eventually known as *chocolatl*, was clearly the beverage of choice in Montezuma's royal household. Over two thousand flasks a day were consumed by this privileged group, and there are stories of Montezuma sending runners to fetch snow from the nearby mountains for a cold and frosty chocolate ice.

When Cortez set sail for Spain, his booty included the precious *cacao* beans and the know-how to make this revolutionary elixir. The Spaniards guarded their new commodity closely, but it wasn't long before enterprising travelers smuggled the dark brown beans into their own countries. By the mid-1600s, this tiny bean had conquered all of Europe and was on its way back to the New World colonies.

For centuries, chocolate was primarily enjoyed as a beverage. Its properties were legendary. Montezuma drank a goblet as an aphrodisiac before entering his harem, and Casanova preferred it over champagne, while Brillat-Savarin, the famous nineteenth century French jurist, writer and gastronome, used it as a mild tranquilizer in his older years. War-minded Aztecs and Napoleon's soldiers swigged it as a bracer, while patrician ladies sipped it as a tonic capable of facilitating weight-gain or loss. Doctors had no trouble prescribing this pleasant panacea.

Science has identified two, similar organic compounds that may explain chocolate's stimulating effects. The more common, caffeine, is a familiar daily drug for those who drink coffee or cola, but the amount of caffeine obtained from a chocolate is much less than that available in a cup of coffee. The second organic compound, theobromine, acts mainly as a diuretic.

Although the evidence is not conclusive, chocolate may also affect the body's level of a naturally occurring amphetamine. An attraction for chocolate may actually have a therapeutic root.

It is only recently in American culinary history that chocolate has become so popular. Nineteenth century cookbooks had only a few recipes devoted to chocolate, and it wasn't until World War I that the chocolate candy bar became popular as a D-ration.

Today, we continue to salute chocolate's seductive powers with Valentine boxes full of truffles and fudge. For stamina, we slip chocolate-chip cookies and brownies in our backpacks and lunch sacks, and at night there's nothing more comforting than a mug of hot chocolate before slipping under the covers and turning out the light.

This small volume is a treasure chest of traditional recipes, tools and tips, so you can make delectable chocolate desserts.

CLASSIFYING CHOCOLATE

For the home cook, unsweetened chocolate, semisweet chocolate and cocoa powder are the three basic chocolates used to create a constellation of chocolate desserts. Their differences are basically determined by the amount of chocolate liquor, cocoa butter and sugar included in each. All three have one essential ingredient: chocolate liquor. This thick liquid is produced when roasted kernels, called nibs, have been finely ground. The liquor naturally contains the essence of cacao and cocoa butter. Sometimes this butter is separated out, because the type of chocolate requires more or less fat.

Listed below you'll find the types of chocolate used in this book's recipes, plus a few extras, with a brief description of what they are and how they are used.

Unsweetened or Baking Chocolate is the basic chocolate from which all others are made. As children, most of us have tasted this bitter form of chocolate when we sneaked into the kitchen to nibble a piece from the tempting brown box. It happens only once. After our first bite, we know this is not the sweet chocolate of our dreams.

The simplest form of chocolate available, unsweetened or baking chocolate is hardened chocolate liquor that has been molded into blocks. According to the United States Standard of Identity, baking chocolate must contain between 50 and 58% cocoa butter. (That's the same percentage found within the roasted cocoa nib.) If you keep it well wrapped in a cool, dry place, it will last indefinitely, unless you have a craving for fudge, or a horde of curious children on the sly.

Semisweet and Bittersweet Chocolate have the intense flavor of chocolate but are slightly sweeter. You have an endless selection of brands, both foreign and domestic from which to choose. For cooking purposes, semisweet and bittersweet are interchangeable. Each contains at least 35% chocolate liquor, plus extra cocoa butter to give a smoother taste and make melting easier. They also contain sugar. Both of these chocolates have a long shelf life, if well wrapped and stored in a cool, dry place.

A word about *chocolate chips:* Even though grocery shelves are stocked with all kinds of seasoned varieties, the most popular chips are still made from semisweet chocolate. Many cooks believe that chocolate chips are endlessly versatile, but remember, they are formulated to tolerate high heat and cookie sheets without melting or scorching. That's good when it comes to your favorite cookie, but may not be so good if you substitute chips for semisweet cooking chocolate in certain recipes.

Cocoa Powder should always be included on anyone's list of kitchen staples. A convenient, durable and inexpensive way of getting a rich chocolate flavor in baked goods, cocoa powder is pulverized chocolate liquor with some of the cocoa butter pressed out. Its cocoa butter varies from 10 to 24%, and it is the one type of chocolate that will work when you discover half-way through a recipe that you won't have enough melted chocolate. If the recipe calls for 1 ounce of unsweetened chocolate, simply use 3 tablespoons of cocoa powder to 1 tablespoon of cooking oil or melted shortening. For semisweet, add 1 tablespoon of granulated sugar. *Dutch-process* cocoa refers to a type of cocoa powder that has been treated with an alkali to make it more soluble. This process gives the cocoa a soft, delicate flavor.

Milk Chocolate may be America's candy bar star, but, except for decorative use, it doesn't work well in most recipes and shouldn't be used as a substitute for baking chocolate. When you realize it needs to contain only 10% chocolate liquor, you know why it plays a minor role in baking. Since milk chocolate does not store well, you are advised to satisfy your cravings promptly.

White Chocolate isn't really chocolate at all, because it contains no chocolate liquor. It does contain cocoa butter with sugar and milk added. Europeans have enjoyed its creamy texture and subtle flavor for years. White chocolate does not work as a substitute for other chocolates in baking. It does not keep well either, so it's best to buy only the amount called for in a recipe.

In other books, you may see a recipe requiring *couverture chocolate*. Because of its high cocoa butter content, professional candymakers use it for dipping. It can be found through specialty cooking stores and wholesalers.

Cooking is one of life's joys. Chocolate is one of life's pleasures. The following information and baking tips will help you take advantage of your resources and get the most out of your efforts.

Melting Chocolate

To melt chocolate, all you really need is patience, perfectly dry utensils and low, uniform heat.

There's a reason to be a stickler about using dry utensils. Chocolate responds noticeably to small amounts of moisture. Whenever you melt chocolate by itself, any moisture less than 1 tablespoon per ounce of chocolate will cause the chocolate to seize— to become grainy and clotted. Even the smallest drop of condensation will have this effect, and that's one reason why you never put the lid on a pan of melting chocolate. (Adding alcohol directly to melting chocolate can also cause seizing.)

If the unfortunate does occur, before you toss out the lumpy mess, try whisking in a teaspoon of vegetable oil or shortening for each ounce of chocolate. The chocolate will often smooth itself out, and the added oil won't alter your recipe. (Do not try this with butter or margarine since they both contain water.)

If you take the time to melt chocolate over low heat, your results will be smooth and silky. Remember, you aren't trying to cook the chocolate, you simply want to get that wonderful flavor in fluid form. Keep chocolate's temperature below 120 degrees. Any higher and its flavor is altered and it can easily burn. One way to accelerate melting is by grating or chopping the chocolate—with a dry grater or knife—to give it more surface area. When it comes to actually melting chocolate, there are several methods you can use.

A *double boiler* is the safest way to melt all types of chocolate. Just be sure to keep the water level in the bottom pan at least ½-inch below the top pan. Keep the water at a low simmer.

Direct heat works well if you're melting chocolate with other ingredients. Using a heavy saucepan over low heat, make sure to stir the chocolate to help prevent scorching. (I use a wooden spoon and occasionally a good quality rubber scraper to keep the chocolate moving while it melts.)

A *microwave* is quickly becoming the favorite appliance for melting chocolate because it's clean and quick. It's best to play it safe and melt at 50% power, checking the chocolate frequently after the first minute. Curiously, when you melt chocolate in a microwave, it often retains its original shape so you can't tell by peering through the window if it's melted or not. Open the door and give it a stir.

A *water bath* works well when you have a small amount of chocolate to melt. Just place the chocolate pieces in a small bowl or custard cup and place the bowl in a pan of hot, shallow water. Since you can do this without a stove, it's a good method to use when your baking partner is a young child. Just be careful none of the water gets into the cup, or your chocolate will seize.

STORING CHOCOLATE

To keep chocolate fresh, always store it in a cool, dry place. A grayish-white film on your chocolate means temperature fluctuations occurred during storage, and the cocoa butter has melted. This is known as bloom and does not affect the quality of the chocolate. (For more information about storing specific chocolates, read *Classifying Chocolates.*)

Baking Tips

The first tip is the one every teacher gave you before a final exam—*read the recipe's instructions before you start.*

Be precise when you measure ingredients. Make sure your measurements are level.

Sift dry ingredients such as flour, cocoa and powdered sugar when the recipe calls for it. Sifting will separate any clumps and will aerate the particles so they are able to mix easily with liquids and produce a lighter texture.

Buy the freshest eggs possible. Make sure their shells are clean and show no signs of cracks. Bacteria which may cause food poisoning can grow in raw eggs. The government has issued warnings about using raw or slightly cooked eggs. I have never had a bad experience using raw eggs, but you use them at your own risk.

Separate eggs fresh from the refrigerator, when they're still chilled. Then let them warm to room temperature since it's better to beat them when they are warm. If you are going to beat whole eggs and you forget to take them out of the refrigerator in time, simply place them intact in a bowl of warm water for several minutes.

Set your oven at the correct temperature at least 15 minutes before you use it. To make sure the temperature is correct, invest in a small oven thermometer.

They're inexpensive—you can purchase them in hardware or specialty cooking stores—and you'll avoid many a ruined cake or soufflé.

Cook most baked goods in the center of the oven, and don't overcrowd. You'll get much better results with an even distribution of heat.

Buy, beg, or borrow a double boiler. It's indispensable for cooking delicate ingredients, like chocolate. Make sure the two pans fit snugly together. If steam or water touches your chocolate, it will seize and may be ruined. (For such an emergency, see *Melting Chocolate*.) If you are really in a jam and can't get your hands on a double boiler, substitute a stainless steel bowl that fits tightly over a saucepan.

Wooden spoons are essential in the kitchen. They feel good in your hand, and they are non-conductive and non-reactive. (With certain acidic ingredients, metal spoons can cause flavor changes and discolorations.)

Baking sheets should be heavy. If not, they'll warp in the oven, along with whatever you're baking. Thin sheets also contribute to uneven baking.

Parchment paper is a godsend. Available in larger grocery chains and specialty cooking stores, this stiff, non-sticky paper has multiple uses in the kitchen. It will line baking sheets, keep a counter clean while sifting and transporting sifted ingredients or operate as a cone for use as a decorating tool. If you're unable to locate a supply, you can grease cookie sheets and use wax paper for lining cake pans.

Depend on your own good sense. As you prepare recipes, nibble on the batter. You'll get to know what you like, or what you might want to try next time, maybe more nuts, maybe none, perhaps a little less sugar. You are also the best judge of when something has finished baking. Ovens are different, so note on your recipe how long the chocolate chip cookies took to bake just the way you like them.

COOKIES

RANDY'S CHOCOLATE MACAROONS

The good news is these chewy macaroons are a breeze to make. The bad news is they won't last long—they get eaten far too quickly!

2 large egg whites, at room temperature

½ cup granulated sugar

Pinch of salt

1½ squares (1½ ounces) bittersweet
  chocolate, melted

2½ cups shredded coconut

Preheat the oven to 325 degrees.

I n the bowl of an electric mixer, combine the egg whites, sugar and salt. Beat until stiff peaks form, about 5 minutes. Remove the beaters. Fold the melted chocolate into the stiffened whites. Do the same with the coconut.

Drop by tablespoonfuls on a parchment-lined baking sheet, 1½ inches apart. Bake for 20 minutes, or until firm and set. Cool for 5 minutes on the baking sheet before transferring to a wire rack, or simply pull the parchment paper from the sheet and place it, along with the cookies, on the wire rack.

Makes 1 dozen cookies.

CHOCOLATE CHIP COOKIES

Ruth Wakefield had no idea she had created a national treasure when she ran out of chopped nuts for her favorite butter cookie recipe and substituted a broken chocolate bar. It was the 1930s, and she had baked the first chocolate chip cookie. Since then, whole cookbooks have been devoted to perfecting chocolate chip cookies.

2¼ cups all-purpose flour

¼ teaspoon salt

1 cup soft butter

1 cup granulated sugar

½ cup light brown sugar, firmly packed

1½ teaspoons vanilla

2 large eggs

1 teaspoon baking soda

1 teaspoon hot water

12 ounces (2 cups) semisweet chocolate chips

Preheat the oven to 350 degrees.

ift together the flour and salt and set aside.

In a large bowl, cream the butter, granulated sugar and brown sugar with a wooden spoon until light and fluffy. Blend in the vanilla. Add the eggs one at a time, mixing well until blended. Add one cup of the flour mixture until it is blended and no flour shows.

In a small cup, dissolve the baking soda in the hot water and mix it into the dough. Add the remaining dry ingredients and blend until no flour shows. *Do not over mix.* Gently stir in the chocolate chips. Cover and refrigerate the dough for 2 hours.

Drop by tablespoonfuls on an ungreased or parchment-lined baking sheet, leaving 2 inches between each mound of dough. Bake in the center of the oven for 14 minutes until the centers are golden. Do not overbake. Cool for several minutes on the baking sheet before transferring to a wire rack, or carefully pull the parchment paper from the pan and place it, along with the cookies, on the wire rack.

Makes 4 dozen cookies.

Variation: For a California Chocolate Chip, sift 1 teaspoon of cinnamon with the flour, add the zest of 1 orange to the egg mixture before adding the dry ingredients, and substitute orange juice for the hot water. Proceed as directed.

COWGIRL COOKIES

Crisp on the outside and chewy on the inside, these oatmeal chocolate chip cookies will drive any cowpuncher or roughrider straight toward the chuckwagon. Home on the range is always more pleasant when these cowgirls are around.

3 cups all-purpose flour

2 teaspoons baking soda

2 teaspoons salt

2 cups butter, or margarine

2 cups granulated sugar

2 cups light brown sugar, firmly packed

2 teaspoons vanilla

4 large eggs

6 cups rolled oats

2½ cups (18 ounces) semisweet chocolate chips

Preheat the oven to 350 degrees.

Sift together the flour, baking soda and salt and set aside.

In a large bowl, cream the butter, granulated sugar and brown sugar with a wooden spoon until light and fluffy. Blend in the vanilla. Add the eggs and mix until blended. Add the sifted, dry ingredients one cup at a time until blended and no flour shows. Add the oats and stir in the chocolate chips.

Drop by tablespoonfuls onto an ungreased or parchment-lined baking sheet, leaving 2 inches between each mound of dough. Bake for 12 minutes, or until golden brown. Cool for several minutes on the baking sheet before transferring to a wire rack, or carefully pull the parchment paper from the pan and place it, along with the cookies, on the wire rack.

Makes 6 dozen cookies.

Variations: For a more voluptuous cookie, increase the flour to 4 cups and substitute 5 cups finely ground rolled oats for the 4 cups rolled oats. (Grind the oats in your blender.) Increase the chips to 24 ounces of semisweet chocolate chips and add one 8-ounce plain chocolate bar, finely grated. Proceed as directed.

For a softer cookie, shape dough into rolls 2 inches in diameter. Refrigerate overnight and cut into ½-inch rounds. Bake at 400 degrees for 6 to 8 minutes. For a crisper cookie, cut into ¼-inch rounds and proceed as directed.

WHAT-COULD-BE-BETTER BROWNIES

If you like dark, rich brownies, these are for you. Served warm from the pan with a scoop of vanilla ice cream and hot fudge sauce, they're my idea of bliss.

4 squares (4 ounces) unsweetened chocolate

½ cup (1 stick) unsalted butter

½ cup all-purpose flour

¼ teaspoon salt

2 large eggs

1 cup granulated sugar

½ teaspoon vanilla

1 cup coarsely chopped walnuts

16 walnut halves

Preheat the oven to 350 degrees.

In a double boiler, melt the chocolate and butter over low heat, blending with a wooden spoon. Set aside to cool.

Sift the flour and salt and set aside.

In a mixing bowl, beat the eggs with the sugar until thick and lemony in color. Add the vanilla. With a few, swift strokes, blend in the chocolate mixture. Add the flour mixture until just blended and no flour shows. Stir in the chopped nuts.

Spread the batter in a greased and floured 8 × 8 × 2-inch pan and space the walnut halves on top in 4 equal rows, so that when the brownies are cut there will be a walnut in the center of each brownie. Bake for 25 minutes until brownies form crust. Cool on a wire rack for 30 minutes and cut in squares.

Makes 16 brownies.

Variation: If you enjoy the taste of raisins in your brownies, decrease the chopped nuts to ½ cup and add ½ cup raisins. Proceed as directed.

CHOCOLATE SHORTBREAD

These are lovely cookies to look at, and they have a wonderful scent. They are lightly flavored with almond and go well with a sophisticated dessert or a glass of icy, cold milk.

1 cup unsalted butter

3/4 cup granulated sugar

1 1/2 teaspoons almond extract

1/4 cup cocoa powder

2 teaspoons baking powder

3/4 cup cake flour

1 1/4 cups all-purpose flour

2 ounces white chocolate candy bar for topping

I n the bowl of an electric mixer, cream the butter and sugar until light and fluffy. Add the almond extract and blend well.

Sift the cocoa, baking powder, cake flour and all-purpose flour over the butter mixture. Carefully beat the mixture until a dough is formed. Shape the dough into two square or triangular logs, each 1 1/2 inches in diameter, and cover tightly with plastic wrap. Refrigerate for at least 2 hours or overnight.

Preheat the oven to 350 degrees. Line baking sheets with parchment paper.

Remove the dough from the refrigerator and cut with a sharp knife into 1/2-inch-thick slices and place 1 inch apart on baking sheets. Bake the cookies for 10 minutes, or until just set. (If overcooked, they will crack and crumble.) Let the cookies sit on the baking sheet until firm enough to remove with a spatula, or carefully pull the parchment paper from the pan and place it, along with the cookies, on the wire rack.

To frost, melt the candy bar in the top of a double boiler and drizzle over the cooled cookies with the tines of a fork or a wooden skewer. Allow the coating to harden before serving.

Makes 3 dozen cookies.

Variation: For coffee lovers, *Chocolate Espresso Shortbread* is an easy variation. Follow the recipe. After the logs are formed, roll the dough in Coffee Sugar (¼ cup finely ground coffee mixed with 1 cup of granulated sugar) before covering with plastic wrap and proceeding as directed.

CANDIES

FANTASY FUDGE

I, for one, love fudge. It's a little like romance—it's sweet, it's satisfying, it's something we can't get enough of. Sometimes it works out; sometimes it just falls apart. Here's a little chocolate affair that shouldn't disappoint you.

3 tablespoons butter, divided

2 squares (2 ounces) unsweetened chocolate, broken in pieces

2 cups granulated sugar

¾ cup whole milk

1 teaspoon light corn syrup

Pinch of salt

1 teaspoon vanilla

½ cup chopped nuts

Using 1 tablespoon of the butter, grease the sides and bottom of a heavy, 2-quart saucepan. Combine the chocolate, sugar, milk, corn syrup and salt, stirring constantly with a wooden spoon until the mixture comes to a boil. Remove the spoon, insert a candy thermometer and let the mixture cook by itself until it *just* reaches the soft ball stage (234 degrees). Remove the saucepan from the heat and add the remaining butter without stirring. Keep the candy thermometer in the mixture until it cools to 110 degrees. *Do not stir.*

With a clean wooden spoon, barely stir the vanilla into the fudge mixture. Pour the fudge into the bowl of an electric mixer. *Do not scrape the sides* (where sugar crystals may reside). Beat the fudge on medium low until it becomes thick and loses its sheen. This may take 10 to 12 minutes. (See Note.)

Stir in the chopped nuts and spread the fudge on a buttered plate or pan, smoothing it with a spatula or knife. Score in squares while warm. Cut when firm. (I have sometimes chilled it briefly to hasten hardening.) Enjoy it fresh on the spot. It's best eaten the day it's made, but it can be kept for a few days at room temperature, if well wrapped.

Makes about 12 large squares.

Note: The finished consistency of fudge depends on the concentration of water. Small variations can make a noticeable difference. It can become crumbly, if it's boiled too long, or runny, if it's not boiled enough. Beating time, the humidity of the day, and other factors will make your fudge turn out a little differently each time. These subtle variations are part of the challenge and pleasure of making and eating fudge.

Variation: You can add a variety of goodies to your fudge. Children of all ages love miniature marshmallows. Raisins are also great, especially if you've marinated them for several hours in strong coffee or your favorite liqueur or rum.

TURTLES

~~~~~~

Tradition says these confections came from the South, where people take their pleasures slowly. No one can eat a turtle fast.

1 cup granulated sugar

½ cup light corn syrup

¼ cup unsalted butter

1 cup light cream, divided (½ cup heavy cream
    mixed with ½ cup half-and-half)

¼ teaspoon salt

1 teaspoon vanilla

¼ pound pecan halves

8 ounces semisweet chocolate

Butter the sides of a heavy saucepan. Combine the sugar, corn syrup, butter and ½ cup light cream over low heat, stirring constantly with a wooden spoon until the mixture boils. Place a candy thermometer in the saucepan. Slowly add the remaining light cream and continue to boil gently, stirring constantly, until it reaches 245 degrees. Remove immediately and let the caramel mixture stand for 5 minutes. Gently blend in the salt and vanilla.

To make each turtle, place 3 or 4 pecan halves in a small circle on ungreased cookie sheet. When caramel has cooled for 10 minutes drop by spoonfuls on circle of pecans. Place sheet in refrigerator to cool turtles for at least 15 minutes.

Meanwhile, melt the chocolate in a double boiler or microwave. When it has cooled slightly, dip each pecan caramel into the melted chocolate using a fork, or your fingers. Place the coated candy on parchment or waxed paper for 30 minutes to set. They may be eaten before you're ready to serve them!

Makes approximately 32 candies.

Variation: To make *Speedy Turtles*, preheat the oven to 325 degrees. Place 3 or 4 pecan halves in a small circle on a greased cookie sheet. Using purchased, cellophane-wrapped caramels, unwrap and place 2 caramels on each grouping of pecans. Bake for 8 to 10 minutes, until the caramel softens. Remove the pecan caramels from the oven and flatten the candies with a greased spatula. Place the candy on waxed paper to harden and coat with melted chocolate.

Truffles are delightful to make because you can "wrap" this exquisite candy in many different and delectable coatings, giving you ample opportunity to indulge a number of vices. I'm a sucker for cocoa, while my brother prefers finely crushed toffee bars. You may like grated chocolate, coconut, powdered sugar dusted with cinnamon, or nuts, and don't stop there—the list goes on.

½ cup half-and-half or whole milk

¼ cup heavy (whipping) cream

¾ pound (12 ounces) imported bittersweet chocolate, finely chopped

4 tablespoons (½ stick) unsalted butter, softened and cut in pieces

½ cup (about 2 ounces) grated imported, semisweet or white chocolate for coating

½ cup Dutch-process cocoa powder for coating

½ cup finely chopped, toasted nuts for coating

In a 2-quart saucepan, combine the milk and heavy cream and heat until boiling. Remove the pan from the heat and immediately whisk in the chopped chocolate and butter until melted. Stir until completely smooth with a wooden spoon, but don't let the mixture form bubbles. Pour onto a baking sheet covered with parchment paper. Refrigerate for 6 hours, or overnight, until the chocolate is completely firm.

To make truffles, take the chilled pan out of the refrigerator and shape the truffles with a melon baller (or two teaspoons) into rough balls about ¾-inch in diameter. Place the balls on a cookie sheet lined with waxed paper and freeze for 30 minutes, so they are firm enough to handle without melting from the heat of your hands.

Place the grated chocolate, cocoa powder and nuts in separate saucers. Roll the

chocolate balls in one or more of these coatings. Return them to the wax paper and refrigerate. They will keep in the refrigerator for two weeks or in the freezer for a month. To serve, bring them back to room temperature.

Makes about 30 truffles.

Variation: Add 1 ounce of your favorite liqueur to the milk mixture when you add the chocolate and butter. Proceed as directed.

To make *espresso truffles*, whisk in 2 to 3 tablespoons of espresso (not coffee) powder to the milk mixture when you add the chocolate and butter. Proceed as directed.

To form a *dipped truffle*, melt 12 ounces of chopped chocolate in a double boiler. Remove the top saucepan from the double boiler and let the chocolate cool to just above body temperature. Carefully drop the chilled truffle balls into the chocolate, one at a time, and roll to cover completely. Lift each truffle out carefully

with a fork, scraping the excess chocolate off the truffle's bottom on the edge of the pan. Place on a paper-lined baking sheet by carefully pushing each truffle off the tines of the fork with the edge of a paring knife. Refrigerate.

CHOCOLATE-DIPPED STRAWBERRIES

Nothing could be simpler: fresh luscious strawberries and your favorite chocolate.

20 fresh, large strawberries, cleaned,
 with stems
6 squares (6 ounces) bittersweet, semisweet
 or milk chocolate, broken in pieces
1 tablespoon vegetable oil

In the top of a double boiler, heat the chocolate and oil until the chocolate is melted. Stir the mixture to a smooth

consistency. Remove the double boiler from the heat, but keep the pan of melted chocolate over the warm water, to maintain a dipping consistency.

Hold each berry by its stem and dip it until ⅔ of its flesh is covered. Let any excess drip off and place the dipped berry on a parchment-lined baking sheet. Let the chocolate cool and set. This dessert is best enjoyed the day it's made. If you refrigerate the berries, the rich flavors are dulled and the chocolate may become brittle.

Makes 20 strawberries.

Variations: Substitute grapes, seedless orange sections, or even crystallized fruits. Proceed as directed.

To make *Chocolate-Dipped Walnuts*, substitute walnut halves for the fruit, using a fondue fork for dipping. Proceed as directed.

CAKES AND PIES

WACKY CAKE

When I went off to college, my mother gave me a clean set of sheets, a case of dental floss, and Peg Bracken's I Hate to Cook Book. *It was my bible for years, and her simple chocolate cake was the first recipe I ever made for my new, unknown roommates. From that point on, I was always the one assigned dessert—not a bad chore. Taking only minutes to prepare, this dessert is fun to make with a young child, and is a perfect after-class snack.*

1½ cups all-purpose flour

¼ cup cocoa powder

1 teaspoon baking soda

Dash of salt

1 cup granulated sugar

1 teaspoon vanilla

1 tablespoon vinegar

5 tablespoons vegetable oil

1 cup warm water

Powdered sugar

Preheat the oven to 350 degrees.

ift the flour, cocoa, baking soda, salt and sugar into a mixing bowl and set aside.

In a small bowl, blend the vanilla, vinegar, vegetable oil and warm water. Stir this liquid into the dry ingredients and spread in a greased, 9-inch round cake pan.

Bake for 30 minutes, or until a toothpick inserted in the middle comes out clean.

Place on a wire rack and dust with powdered sugar. Serve warm.

If you're in a playful mood or cooking with a child, sift the dry ingredients into a greased, 9-inch round pan. Make a dent with your finger in one corner and add the vanilla. Make a dent with your thumb in the opposite corner and add the vinegar. Draw a line through the

middle of the pan and pour the oil along the line. Pour the water over the entire surface and stir very well until all the ingredients are blended. Proceed as directed.

Makes 1 cake (serves 4 to 6).

SAVANNAH SILK PIE

The sweet graham cracker crust goes especially well with the sumptuously smooth chocolate filling. It's the perfect pie for special family suppers or served all by itself with a steaming cup of French roast or chickory-blended coffee.

Crust

1½ cups fine graham cracker crumbs

3 tablespoons granulated sugar

⅓ cup butter, melted

Filling

3 ounces unsweetened chocolate

¾ cup soft butter

1 cup granulated sugar

2 teaspoons vanilla

3 large eggs

1 cup heavy cream, whipped

Chocolate curls for garnish, optional (see Note)

Preheat the oven to 325 degrees.

In a mixing bowl, combine the graham cracker crumbs, sugar and melted butter. Press the mixture into the bottom and sides of a 9-inch pie pan. Bake the crust for 10 to 12 minutes. Cool on a wire rack and chill for 1 hour.

To prepare the filling, melt the chocolate in the top of a double boiler. Set aside to cool slightly.

Cream the butter and sugar with an electric mixer until light and fluffy. Beat in the vanilla and melted chocolate. Add the eggs one at a time, beating at medium high speed 5 minutes after each egg. Pour the filling into the chilled shell and return to the refrigerator until set.

Before serving, cover the top of the pie with whipped cream, piped or spooned. Garnish with chocolate curls.

Makes 1 pie.

Note: To make *chocolate curls*, unwrap your favorite chocolate candy bar and let it soften to room temperature. Hold the bar with a piece of toweling or wax paper so the warmth of your hand won't melt it. Pulling a sharp potato peeler along the horizontal side of the bar, press firmly against the chocolate in long, thin strokes, creating curls as you go.

MUD-IN-YOUR-EYE PIE

Mud pie has everything a chocolate lover could want—chocolate crust, chocolate ice cream and chocolate sauce. It can't get much better than this!

Crust

1 cup plain chocolate wafer crumbs

1 cup graham cracker crumbs

4 tablespoons butter, melted

Filling

1 quart dark chocolate or coffee ice cream,
   slightly softened

2 squares (2 ounces) unsweetened chocolate

2 tablespoons butter

½ cup sugar

Pinch of salt

¾ cup heavy (whipping) cream

¼ cup diced or slivered toasted almonds
   (see Note)

Topping

1 cup heavy (whipping) cream

2 tablespoons powdered sugar

To prepare the crust, toss the chocolate wafer crumbs and graham cracker crumbs in a mixing bowl. Add the melted butter and mix well. Use your fingers to press the crumb mixture evenly over the bottom and sides of a 9-inch pie pan. Freeze for ½ hour.

Spread the ice cream evenly over the crust, mounding slightly in the center, and place in the freezer for at least 2 hours.

In the top of a double boiler, melt the chocolate and butter. Remove the double boiler from the heat and mix in the sugar and salt, stirring with a wooden spoon for 2 minutes. Add ¾ cup of heavy cream and return the double boiler to the heat, cooking until the mixture is smooth, about 5 minutes. Remove from the heat and chill thoroughly.

Spread the chocolate mixture over the ice cream and sprinkle with toasted nuts. Return to the freezer.

When you are ready to eat the pie, whip the 1 cup of heavy cream, adding 1 tablespoon of the powdered sugar at a time, until peaks are firm. Serve the whipped cream on the side.

Makes 1 pie (serves 8).

Note: To toast *almonds*, preheat the oven to 350 degrees. Spread whole, slivered, or sliced almonds on a baking sheet. Bake in the center of the oven, stirring occasionally, until they are golden, about 8 to 10 minutes.

Park Avenue Chocolate Cheesecake

While helping a friend move into an old brownstone, I came across a piece of folded, green steno paper, blotted with melted chocolate, butter and coffee rings. Just before throwing it away, I unfolded the note and found this gem.

Crust

¾ cup graham cracker crumbs

½ cup chocolate wafer crumbs

2 tablespoons granulated sugar

3 tablespoons butter, melted

Filling

8 ounces semisweet chocolate

3 tablespoons heavy (whipping) cream

1½ pounds cream cheese, softened

2 cups granulated sugar

3 large eggs

1 cup sour cream

¼ cup dark rum

¾ teaspoon cinnamon

¾ teaspoon almond extract

Topping

¾ cup sour cream

¾ cup powdered sugar

¾ teaspoon vanilla

Grated chocolate for garnish

> *or edible flowers—pansies, violets,*

> *nasturtiums—(clean and pesticide-free)*

Preheat the oven to 300 degrees.

In a small bowl, mix the graham cracker crumbs, wafer crumbs, sugar and melted butter. Firmly press in the bottom of a 9-inch springform pan.

To prepare filling, melt the chocolate and the heavy cream in a double boiler. Blend with a wooden spoon. Set aside to cool.

In the bowl of an electric mixer, beat the cream cheese until light and fluffy. Gradually add the sugar and beat until

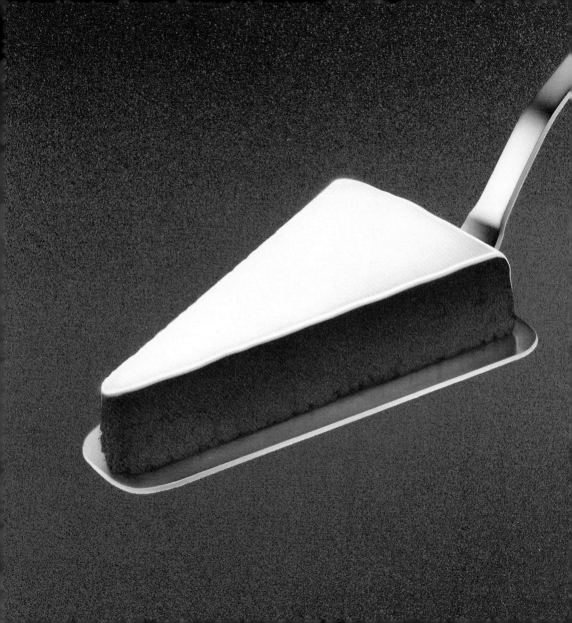

fluffy. Add the eggs, one at a time, and blend until smooth. Beat in the melted chocolate and the sour cream. Add the rum, cinnamon and almond extract and beat the mixture until smooth and creamy, about 2 minutes.

Pour the mixture into the prepared crust and bake for 1 hour until the center is firm. Allow it to cool to room temperature. Loosen the edge of the cheesecake with a knife before removing the sides of the pan.*

To prepare topping, combine the sour cream, powdered sugar, and vanilla and blend until smooth. Spread over the slightly cooled cheesecake. Refrigerate the cake for 6 hours or overnight. To protect the cheesecake while it's being chilled, replace the sides of the spring-form pan. This also makes it easier to cover the top with foil or plastic wrap.

Serve in small wedges and garnish as desired.

Makes 1 cheesecake.

*If the top is uneven, you can trim it with a knife.

SCHOOL-YARD CUPCAKES

This is one cupcake kids actually like without frosting. You can slip one into a sandwich bag without any smushed complaints. But for those back-to-school meetings and afternoon soccer games, I've included a yummy frosting complete with jimmies, gumdrops or chocolate-dipped nuts.

Cupcakes

1³/4 cups all-purpose flour

³/4 teaspoon baking soda

¹/4 teaspoon salt

3 squares (3 ounces) unsweetened chocolate

¹/2 cup butter

1¹/2 cups granulated sugar

1 teaspoon vanilla

2 large eggs

1 cup sour cream

Frosting

2 cups heavy (whipping) cream
1/2 cup cocoa powder
1/2 cup granulated sugar
Pinch of salt
Jimmies, gum drops, chocolate-dipped walnut
    halves (see Page 32) for garnish

Preheat the oven to 375 degrees. Line a medium muffin pan with paper liners.

Sift the flour, baking soda and salt and set aside.

Melt the chocolate in a double boiler or a microwave and set aside.

In a mixing bowl, cream the butter and sugar with a wooden spoon until light and fluffy. Blend in the vanilla. Add the eggs and beat until fluffy. Blend in the melted chocolate. Add the sifted ingredients and sour cream in thirds to the butter mixture, beating well after each addition. Continue beating for 1 minute.

Pour the batter into the paper-lined muffin cups, filling each 1/2 full. Bake for 20 minutes, or until a wood toothpick inserted in the center comes out clean. Cool on a wire rack.

To make frosting, combine the heavy cream, cocoa powder, sugar and salt in a 2-quart saucepan. Gently heat and stir continuously until the sugar has dissolved and the cocoa is blended. Remove from heat and chill.

Strain the chilled mixture into a bowl and whip until the frosting is smooth and has a spreading consistency. (It will be quite firm.) Frost and garnish with jimmies, gumdrops or chocolate-dipped walnut halves.

Makes 18 cupcakes.

HAPPY BIRTHDAY CAKE

Anyone's birthday will be made happy with this chocolate cake. There's enough rich frosting for the most ardent icing lover.

Cake

1¾ cups flour

½ teaspoon baking powder

1¼ teaspoons baking soda

Pinch of salt

½ cup butter, melted

2 large eggs

1 cup buttermilk

2 cups granulated sugar

¾ cup Dutch-process cocoa powder

1 teaspoon vanilla

Frosting

½ cup boiling water

4 tablespoons instant coffee

¾ pound (3 sticks) unsalted butter

¼ pound (1 stick) salted butter

4½ ounces Dutch-process cocoa

1 pound (1 box) powdered sugar

1 large egg

1 teaspoon vanilla

½ cup (3.5 ounces) chocolate sprinkles
  for garnish

Preheat the oven to 350 degrees. Butter and flour two 9-inch cake pans. Line the bottom of each with waxed or parchment paper and butter and flour the paper.

Sift together the flour, baking powder, baking soda and salt. Set aside.

In the bowl of an electric mixer, combine the butter, eggs, buttermilk, sugar, cocoa and vanilla and continue to beat for 3 minutes until well blended. With the mixer on low speed, add the sifted flour mixture until completely blended.

Turn the batter into the prepared pans and tap once to settle the batter. Bake for 30 minutes, or until a toothpick inserted in the center comes out clean. Cool the cakes in their pans for 10 minutes before inverting on wire racks. Cool thoroughly before frosting.

To make frosting, combine the water and instant coffee in a small bowl. Stir to dissolve, and set aside to cool.

Cream all the butter in the large bowl of an electric mixer on medium speed for several minutes. Combine the cocoa and sugar in a sifter and sift the mixture, ⅓ at a time, into the butter, beating well after each addition. (Careful, some of the cocoa may fly into the air.) Add the egg and vanilla and beat for 30 seconds. Add the coffee and beat for 5 minutes. The frosting will lighten in color and become fluffy.

To assemble cake, place a dollop of icing in the middle of your serving platter. Place the bottom layer on the platter, top-side down, securing its position with the icing. Spread half of the frosting on the bottom layer of the cooled cake. Place the top layer on top of the frosting and spread the remaining frosting on the top and sides. Garnish the top and sides with chocolate sprinkles.

Makes 1 cake (serves 10 to 12).

ICE CREAMS, PUDDINGS
AND SAUCES

CHOCOLATE SAUCE

Served over ice cream, cake, or pudding, this rich and satiny sauce is wonderfully versatile.

6 ounces bittersweet chocolate, broken in pieces

1/3 cup granulated sugar

Dash of salt

2/3 cup boiling water

1/2 teaspoon vanilla

In the top of a double boiler, melt the chocolate. Remove the double boiler from the heat and mix in the sugar and salt, stirring for 1 minute. Pour in the boiling water and stir until there is no graininess left and the sugar is completely dissolved. (It's helpful to use a rubber spatula to scrape down the sides of the pan.)

Return to the heat and cook until the mixture slightly thickens, about 2 minutes. Remove from the heat and stir in the vanilla.

Store in airtight containers in the refrigerator. To serve, reheat over low heat or in a microwave.

Variations: Flavored chocolate sauces are made by adding 1/2 teaspoon of extract (such as almond or peppermint) to the sauce at the same time the vanilla is added. Proceed as directed.

For a crunchy dessert sauce, add 2/3 cup coarsely chopped walnuts, hazelnuts or other nutmeats to the sauce. Crushed peppermint or toffee candy can also be added after the sauce has cooled slightly.

Makes 1 1/2 cups sauce.

CHOCOLATE VELVET ICE CREAM

A dessert to satisfy anyone's sweet tooth, this double-chocolate ice cream will make a fabulous finale to your next dinner party. If you're lucky enough to have any left, save it to create a truly decadent hot fudge sundae or to give a simple ice cream soda a whole new persona. There are no preservatives in homemade ice cream, so enjoy it soon after you make it.

¼ cup Dutch-process cocoa powder

2 cups (3.8%) milk, divided

¼ cup brown sugar, firmly packed

4 ounces imported, bittersweet chocolate

4 large egg yolks

¾ cup granulated sugar

In a 2-quart saucepan, combine the cocoa and ¼ cup milk and stir with a wooden spoon until the mixture forms a smooth paste. Whisk in the remaining milk and brown sugar, stirring to dissolve. Add the chocolate and place the saucepan over low heat, stirring with a wooden spoon until the chocolate has melted and the mixture is steaming. *Do not allow it to boil.*

Meanwhile, beat the egg yolks and granulated sugar until they are creamy and a pale lemony color.

Slowly add the chocolate mixture to the beaten eggs, return to the 2-quart saucepan and place over low heat. Cook, stirring constantly until the custard thickens and covers the back of a spoon. *Do not allow it to come near a boil.*

Strain the custard through a fine sieve into a glass or plastic container. Cool, cover and refrigerate overnight. Place the chilled custard mixture in your ice cream maker and follow manufacturer's instructions.

Makes 1½ quarts.

CHOCOLATE CHIP ICE CREAM

This is one of the best chocolate chip ice creams I've ever tasted. Half the fun of making this ice cream is watching the warmed, bittersweet chocolate form ribbons of "chips" in the rich vanilla custard. I'm halfway tempted each time I make this recipe not to freeze the whole batch, but to keep some refrigerated for an interesting soft custard sauce spooned over bread pudding or fresh fruit.

2 cups whole milk

2 cups heavy (whipping) cream

1 cup granulated sugar, divided

Pinch of salt

10 large egg yolks

1 tablespoon vanilla

3 ounces bittersweet chocolate

In a 2-quart saucepan, combine the milk, cream, ½ cup granulated sugar, and pinch of salt over low heat. Stir with a wooden spoon until the sugar has dissolved and the mixture is steaming. *Do not allow it to boil.*

Meanwhile, beat the egg yolks and the remaining ½ cup granulated sugar until creamy and a pale lemony color.

Slowly add the milk and cream mixture to the egg mixture until blended, return to the 2-quart saucepan and place over low heat. Cook, stirring constantly with a wooden spoon, until the custard thickens and covers the back of the spoon. *Do not allow it to come near a boil.*

Strain the custard through a fine sieve into a glass or plastic container. Stir in the vanilla. Cover with plastic wrap and refrigerate overnight.

In the top of a double boiler, or in a bowl in a microwave, melt the chocolate. When the chocolate has melted and is still warm, pour a portion at a time into the custard and whisk briskly to form "chips." Place the mixture in your ice cream maker and follow manufacturer's instructions.

Makes 1½ quarts.

HOMER'S HOT FUDGE SAUCE

Just what you want in a hot fudge sauce: it turns chewy the moment it hits your favorite ice cream. Fudge sauce can be refrigerated for up to 10 days, but it needs to be reheated and served warm or hot.

6 ounces semisweet chocolate, broken in pieces

¼ cup unsalted butter

½ cup granulated sugar

Pinch of salt

3 tablespoons Dutch-process cocoa powder

¾ cup heavy (whipping) cream

½ teaspoon vanilla

In the top of a double boiler, melt the chocolate and butter. Remove the double boiler from the heat and mix in the sugar and salt, stirring for 2 minutes with a wooden spoon. (Mixture will look thick and granular.) Blend in the cocoa and heavy cream and return the double boiler to the heat, stirring until the mixture is smooth and heated through, about 5 minutes. Remove from the heat and stir in the vanilla.

Store in airtight containers in the refrigerator.

Makes 1½ cups sauce.

MARTHA WHEATON'S OLD-FASHIONED CHOCOLATE PUDDING

My mother makes the best chocolate pudding I've ever tasted. Its rich, thick, chocolaty flavor makes it a family favorite. It's the first thing my college-age son, Matthew, asks for when he's home on vacation. As the pudding cools in the refrigerator, it forms a dark, thin crust—that's the best part!

2 tablespoons milk

3/4 cup granulated sugar

1/4 teaspoon salt

6 tablespoons flour

3 squares (3 ounces) unsweetened chocolate,
    broken in pieces

3 cups evaporated milk

1 large egg, slightly beaten

1 teaspoon vanilla

Sweetened, whipped cream for garnish

I n a small bowl, make a paste of the milk, sugar, salt and flour. Set aside.

In a double boiler, combine the chocolate and evaporated milk and stir with a wooden spoon until the chocolate has melted. Add the paste to the heated chocolate mixture and cook until thickened, about 10 minutes. Then add the slightly beaten egg to the chocolate mixture at the last minute when it is still cooking in the double boiler. Remove from heat and stir in the vanilla. Pour into a clear, glass bowl or individual bowls. Refrigerate for several hours before serving. To serve, place a generous dollop of whipped cream on each serving.

Makes 4 to 6 servings.

CHOCOLATE BREAD PUDDING WITH VANILLA CREAM

Just right for a lazy weekend brunch, this nostalgic bread pudding makes anyone feel comfortably nourished with its rich chocolate custard. Also perfect as a dinner dessert, its scrumptious taste is perfect after a light summer meal.

Pudding

5 ounces semisweet chocolate, broken in pieces

1½ cups half-and-half

3 tablespoons softened butter, divided

4 tablespoons granulated sugar, divided

10 slices homemade-style white bread,
   ½-inch thick, crusts removed

6 large eggs, beaten lightly

½ teaspoon vanilla

¼ teaspoon salt

Vanilla Cream

1 cup heavy (whipping) cream, chilled

2 tablespoons sifted powdered sugar

2 teaspoons vanilla

In the top of a double boiler, combine chocolate and half-and-half and cook until the chocolate is melted and the mixture is smooth. Remove the double boiler from the heat and set aside.

Using 2 tablespoons of the butter, spread one side of each slice of bread and sprinkle with 2 tablespoons of sugar. Arrange bread, butter-side up, on a cookie sheet and lightly toast under the broiler. Cut the bread in 1-inch cubes. (You should have 6 to 8 cups.) With the remaining 1 tablespoon of butter, grease a 9-inch, deep-dish pie pan. Place half of the bread cubes in the pan.

In a large bowl, whisk the eggs, remaining sugar, vanilla and salt. Whisk in the warm, chocolate liquid. Pour half this mixture over the cubes in the deep-dish pie pan. Let rest for 10 minutes to absorb liquid. Add the remaining cubes and add the remaining liquid. Let the pan stand for 15 to 20 minutes.

Set the deep-dish pan in a larger pan and add enough hot water to the outer pan to come halfway up the side of the baking dish. Bake in the center of the oven for 45 minutes until the custard is set. (A knife inserted in the center of the pudding should come out clean.) Cool on a wire rack for 15 minutes.

To make the vanilla cream, whip the cream, adding 1 tablespoon of powdered sugar and 1 teaspoon of vanilla at a time until soft peaks form. Spoon the whipped cream on top or serve separately in a bowl.

Makes 6 servings.

A Continental Sampling

Radio crooner Harry Babbitt and his wife, Betty, had a houseful of sons, and every Christmas their friends came over to decorate the tree. There was always a table of chocolate delights, and éclairs were a favorite. A festive treat any time of year, this recipe gives you a double chocolate treat with its delectable chocolate pastry cream.

Pastry

8 tablespoons (1 stick) unsalted butter

1 1/3 cups water

1 1/3 cups all-purpose flour, sifted

Pinch of salt

1 teaspoon vanilla

4 large eggs

Filling

3 ounces (3 squares) semisweet chocolate

1 tablespoon all-purpose flour

2 teaspoons cornstarch

1 tablespoon granulated sugar

1 large egg

1 1/2 cups (3.8%) milk

Glaze

1 square (1 ounce) unsweetened chocolate

1 teaspoon unsalted butter

1 cup powdered sugar, sifted

2 tablespoons hot water

Preheat the oven to 400 degrees.

In a large saucepan, combine the butter and water. Cook over medium heat until the mixture boils. Add the flour and salt, all at once, and stir over high heat until the dough pulls away from the sides of the pan.

Place the dough in the bowl of an electric mixer and beat on medium for 4 minutes. Add the vanilla and eggs, one at a time, mixing until well blended.

To shape the éclairs, place the dough in a pastry bag fitted with a plain, ½-inch nozzle. Pipe out in fingers, 4½ inches long and 1½ inches wide, and place 2 inches apart on parchment-lined baking sheets. (Or, take approximately ¼ cup dough and shape into a finger.) Brush each éclair lightly with water and bake for 20 minutes. Reduce the heat to 350 degrees. Open the oven door and carefully pierce each éclair with a sharp knife (to let steam escape) and continue to bake for another 5 to 7 minutes, until golden. They should sound hollow. Cool on a wire rack. Using a knife, cut each éclair horizontally in half and set aside.

To prepare the filling, melt the chocolate in a double boiler or microwave. Set aside. Combine the flour, cornstarch and sugar in a small bowl. Place the egg in the bowl of an electric mixer and whisk until frothy. Add the flour mixture to the egg and beat at medium speed until they are light in color.

In a large saucepan, bring the milk to a boil. Slowly add the milk to the egg mixture, then return the milk-egg mixture to the saucepan. Over low heat, bring it to a boil, stirring constantly with a whisk. Remove from the heat, add the melted chocolate and stir until smooth and blended. Cool.

Place the cooled filling into a pastry bag fitted with a tube. Pipe in the filling. Repeat until all the éclairs are filled. Arrange on a cookie sheet or tray and place in the refrigerator until ready to glaze.

To make glaze, melt the unsweetened chocolate and butter in a double boiler or microwave. In a mixing bowl, combine the powdered sugar, hot water and chocolate mixture. Beat with a spoon until smooth and slightly thickened.

Frost each éclair and return the glazed éclairs to the refrigerator until ready to serve.

Makes about 12 éclairs and 2 cups of filling.

Variation: For a chocolaty pastry, sift 2 tablespoons cocoa and 1 tablespoon granulated sugar with the flour and salt and proceed as directed.

Friday's Chocolate Mousse

Friday not only hails the weekend, it also signals a great meal and my favorite chocolate mousse. That's our traditional night for dining at L'Auberge, which provided this marvelous recipe.

8 ounces bittersweet chocolate, broken in pieces

1 cup plus 3 tablespoons heavy (whipping) cream, divided

¼ cup sugar syrup (see Note)

2 tablespoons Cognac

2 extra-large egg whites

Pinch of cream of tartar

Lightly sweetened whipped cream for garnish

In a double boiler, melt the chocolate, 3 tablespoons of the heavy cream, the sugar syrup and the Cognac. Gently whisk together until smooth and glossy. Set aside.

Whip the remaining 1 cup of heavy cream until soft peaks form. Set aside.

Whip the egg whites with the cream of tartar until soft peaks form. Gently fold the egg whites into the chocolate mixture until just mixed. Gently fold the whipped cream into the chocolate mixture until well combined. The mixture will be quite soft.

Carefully spoon the mousse into 6 champagne glasses. Chill for 4 hours. Garnish with decoratively piped, lightly sweetened, whipped cream.

Makes 6 servings.

Note: To make a simple *sugar syrup*, combine 1½ cups water and 1 cup plus 2 tablespoons granulated sugar in a medium saucepan. Bring it to a boil over medium heat, and boil until the sugar is dissolved and syrup is clear, about 20 seconds. Cool and store in an air-tight container in the refrigerator.

CHOCOLATE SOUFFLÉ

This is a festive dessert to serve on New Year's Eve with a bottle of your best champagne.

1 tablespoon butter

1 tablespoon granulated sugar

3 ounces semisweet chocolate, broken in pieces

3 ounces unsweetened chocolate, broken in pieces

¾ cup granulated sugar, divided

½ cup half-and-half

6 large eggs, separated

Powdered sugar

Preheat the oven to 375 degrees. (See Note.)

Generously butter a 6-cup soufflé dish. Dust the dish with sugar; tap out excess.

In a heavy saucepan, combine the semi-sweet chocolate, unsweetened chocolate, ½ cup sugar and half-and-half. Place over low heat, stirring constantly, until the chocolate is melted and the mixture is smooth. Pour into a large bowl and let the mixture cool for 10 minutes.

Separate the eggs. Place 4 yolks in one bowl and 6 egg whites in another. (Save the extra 2 yolks for other uses.)

In the bowl of an electric mixer, whisk 4 egg yolks with 2 tablespoons sugar until light and lemon colored. Add the yolk mixture to the chocolate mixture and stir until blended.

In the clean bowl of an electric mixer, combine the 6 egg whites and whisk until soft peaks form. Sprinkle in the remaining 2 tablespoons sugar and whisk until stiff but not dry. Gently fold ¼ of the egg whites into the chocolate mixture. Fold in the remaining whites.

Pour into the prepared soufflé dish. Place the soufflé dish on a baking sheet and bake for 35 minutes, or until soufflé is puffed on top and a knife inserted in the center comes out clean. Dust with powdered sugar and serve immediately.

Makes 1 soufflé (serves 4).

Note: Soufflés demand the correct oven temperature. So, doublecheck with your portable oven thermometer. (See Baking Tips.)

EASY STREET CHOCOLATE FONDUE

Whenever a new family moves into our neighborhood, someone always throws a block party, and this quick and simple dessert is, without exception, the most popular.

Fondue

12 ounces semisweet chocolate

⅔ cup heavy (whipping) cream

*2 tablespoons brandy or orange-flavored
    liqueur*

Dippers, cut into bite-size pieces

strawberries, mandarin orange segments,
grapes, pound cake, biscotti, dried apricots,
peanut brittle, meringues, pineapple chunks,
fresh orange slices, kiwifruit slices, shortbread,
pretzels, nuts, caramels, macaroons

In a 2-quart saucepan, melt the chocolate and heavy cream over low heat, stirring constantly with a wooden spoon. When the mixture is smooth, remove from the heat and stir in the liqueur. Pour the chocolate mixture into a fondue pot or chafing dish, keeping warm over low heat.

Arrange the fondue pot and platter of dippers on a table. Serve with long-handled fondue forks or wooden skewers.

Makes 1¾ cups fondue, enough to serve 6 to 8.

Variation: For children's parties, substitute orange juice for the liqueur. Proceed as directed.

DRINKS

Pharmacy Fountain Chocolate Soda

~~~~~~

This is the perfect reward for good grades and a treat for any small celebrations. Children and adults love its bubbling fizz.

3 tablespoons chilled chocolate-flavored syrup

2 tablespoons chilled whole milk

½ to ¾ cup chilled seltzer water or club soda

1 large scoop vanilla ice cream

Sweetened whipped cream for garnish

Maraschino cherry or chocolate curls for

garnish (see Page 37)

 or each serving, combine the chilled milk and chocolate syrup in a 12-ounce chilled glass. Add the seltzer water to fill the glass ¾ full and stir. Add the vanilla ice cream and top with seltzer water. If you're in an extravagant mood, garnish with sweetened whipped cream and a maraschino cherry or chocolate curls.

Makes 1 serving.

Variations: For a subtle, fruit-flavored soda, decrease the chocolate syrup to 2 tablespoons and substitute fruit-flavored, carbonated spring water. Proceed as directed.

For a more intense chocolate flavor, use chocolate milk and/or chocolate ice cream. Proceed as directed.

Topped with clouds of marshmallows or whipped cream, a steaming cup of hot chocolate is the perfect start for any day. And at night before bed, there's nothing better for sweet dreams.

1 cup heavy (whipping) cream

2 squares (2 ounces) unsweetened chocolate, broken in pieces

2 squares (2 ounces) semisweet chocolate, broken in pieces

¼ cup granulated sugar

½ teaspoon vanilla

3 cups whole milk

Marshmallows or sweetened whipped cream with cinnamon for garnish

I n a 2-quart saucepan, heat the heavy cream to scalding until tiny bubbles form around the edge of the pan. Remove from the heat and stir in the chocolate pieces until they have melted and the mixture is smooth. Add the sugar and vanilla and stir until smooth. Pour in the milk. Return the saucepan to the stove and heat over medium until the mixture is hot and steaming. *Do not bring to a boil.* If you are feeling especially festive, top with marshmallows or whipped cream and sprinkle with cinnamon.

Makes 4 mugs or 6 demitasse servings.

Variation: For *Brazilian Hot Chocolate,* substitute 1½ cups of strong black coffee for the 3 cups of milk. Proceed as directed. Top with whipped cream sprinkled with ground cinnamon and grated orange zest.

DOUBLE-STRAW CHOCOLATE SHAKE

Here's a smooth, cool shake to share with your sweetheart after the movie, or, should a sweetheart not be available, all by yourself.

2 heaping scoops vanilla ice cream

¾ cup chilled (3.8%) milk

⅓ cup chilled, chocolate-flavored syrup

Place the ice cream, chilled milk and chocolate syrup in your blender. Blend until just smooth, or leave chunks of ice cream, whichever you prefer. Pour into a chilled, 12-ounce glass, reserving any extra for a refill. Serve with two straws.

Makes approximately 2 cups.

Variation: For a more intense chocolate flavor, use chocolate milk and / or chocolate ice cream. Proceed as directed.

For the ultimate *Chocolate Malt*, add 2 tablespoons of malted milk powder or 3 tablespoons of chocolate malted milk powder to the blender. Proceed as directed. (Malted milk powders are found in the sugar and syrup section of your grocery.)

INDEX

ACKNOWLEDGMENTS

My thanks go to Emily Moore, my consultant and a preeminent chef in the Pacific Northwest, for her astute advice and unending enthusiasm.

My thanks also go to the friends who generously shared their ideas, time, and kitchens, especially Karen Brooks, Bette Sinclair, Arlene Schnitzer, Lisa Shara Hall, Patty Merrill, Bill McLaughlin, Randy Nicholson, Larry Kirkland, Diana Boom, Lucinda Henry, Jane Mannix, Debby Hopp and to Catherine Gleason, my editor, whose guidance, suggestions and humor continue to make writing a pleasure.

My greatest thanks go to my husband, Pete, who makes it all easy, and my special thanks to Bill LeBlond, senior editor at Chronicle Books, who makes it all possible.